LIFT THEM UP

How to Rise above Bullying and Live an Empowered Life

Self-Defense, Parenting, Self-Help

© Copyright 2018 By: Edward Carr

All rights reserved. No part of this book may be reproduced or transmitted in any form or by any means, electronic or mechanical, including photocopying, recording or by any information storage and retrieval system without written permission of the publisher, except for the inclusion of brief quotations in a review.

Printed in the U.S.A.

Published By:

Ocean View Publishing, LLC

Lift Them Up

How to Rise above Bullying and Live an Empowered Life

Self-Defense, Parenting, Self-Help

ISBN: 978-0-9989928-8-4

DISCLAIMER:

The purpose of this book is to educate and entertain. The author and publisher does not guarantee anyone following the techniques, suggestions, ideas and strategies will become successful. The author and publisher shall have neither, liability nor responsibility to anyone with respect to any loss or damage caused, or alleged to be caused, directly or indirectly by the information contained in this book.

Table of Contents

Introduction 9
Bullying - A Pervasive Threat 1
   School Setting Bullying 2
   Forms of School Bullying 4
   Reasons for School Bullying 5
   Effects of Bullying 6
   Workplace Bullying 7
   Conclusion 8
What Causes Bullying? 9
   Expected and Unexpected Causes 9
   Media Influence 11
   Parents and Other Relatives 12
   Society 13
   Is It Biology? 15
Physical Bullying 17
   Forms of Physical Bullying 17
   Reasons for Physical Bullying 19
   Results of Physical Bullying 20
   Signs of Physical Bullying 21
Cyberbullying 22
   The Different Faces of Cyberbullying 23
   How To Tell If Your Child Is Being Cyberbullied 26
   How To Help Cyberbullying Victims 27
   Other Ways of Fighting Cyberbullying 28
   Conclusion 29
Sexual Bullying 30
   What Constitutes Sexual Bullying? 30

    What Do Sexual Bullies Do? 31

    Reasons for Sexual Bullying 32

    More Thoughts About Someone Who Has Been Sexually Bullied 34

    Conclusion 35

Effects of Bullying 36

    Effects on Those Being Bullied 36

    Effects on Bystanders 38

    Vicarious Harm 39

    Guilt and Shame 39

    Fear and Anxiety 40

    Pressure to Participate 41

    Effects on the Bullies 41

    Countering the Negative Effects 42

Basic Child and Family Safety 44

    Stolen Identity 44

    Phishing Scams 47

    General Safety for the Internet 48

    Conclusions 49

Preventive Programs to Stop Bullying 51

Self-Esteem, Self-Confidence and Bullying 56

    Take Time For Your Kids 57

    Let Them Fail 58

    Give Them Chores and Jobs 58

    Teach Them To Be Assertive 59

    Help Them Learn To Insulate Themselves 60

    Another Way To Build Self-Esteem 61

    Conclusion 62

Self-Discipline and Bullying 63

    What Is Self-Discipline? 63

  Help Them Learn to Receive Correction 65

  Get Them Started On Tasks That Build Self-Discipline 65

  Parent Cautions 66

  A Great Way To Develop Self-Discipline 67

The Importance of Parenting and Communication 68

  Help Them Learn About Bullying 68

  Always Communicate 69

  Listening: The Forgotten Skill 70

  Body Language 70

  Don't Over-React 71

  Some Other Parenting Helps 72

  What About The Parents Of Bullies? 73

The Benefits of Martial Arts Training 75

Take Action 78

About Edward Carr 79

Biography 80

Introduction

I have spent the last 27 years working with kids and families. In that time, the community has come to lean on my ability to help local kids deal with, cope and defend themselves against all types of bullies.

These days bullying has gone so far beyond the stereotypical "schoolyard bully." Bullying reaches far and wide. It impacts kids and adults. It can start early in life. If not handled correctly bullying can have lasting negative effects.

If your child is being bullied, you want to act to help stop it, if possible. There are ways to help your child cope with teasing, bullying, or mean gossip, and lessen its lasting impact. And even if bullying isn't an issue in your house right now, it's important to discuss it so your kids will be prepared if it does happen to them.

This book is my attempt to give back even more to the community that has given so much to me. What we have done here in these pages is aim to get the basic facts out about bullying and introduce some simple strategies parents and kids can use to defend themselves.

There is so much more to this defense than protecting against physical harm. A lot is a stake. The future can be influenced positively if less kids are bullied and less kids engage in bullying others

Bullying - A Pervasive Threat

While anyone who has a child in school, knows someone who has a child in school, or works in a school knows bullying takes place, the vast majority of people who have been bulled don't report the incident(s). Nearly everyone who works either has been bullied at work, knows someone who has been bullied at work, or has witnessed someone being bullied at work. But still most do not report it.

Those who have been bullied seem to feel alone.

But that is certainly not the case. Bullying at school, in the work place, and over social media now is rampant.

Let's take a look at some of the statistics put together by several national organizations dedicated to putting an end to the bullying spreading across our nation. These statistics were gathered from web sites such as pacer.org and nobullying.com.

A study conducted by the Journal of the American Medical Association's Pediatrics Network in 2013 showed 80% of young people who commit suicide did so because of bullying or victimization by their peers.

Another survey conducted in 2013, this one by Knowthenet.org, talked to 2001 teenagers. A startling fact emerged that 37% of cyberbullying victims never reported the bullying. And the older a teen gets, the less likely he or she is to report the incident. In this survey, nearly 85%

of those age 19 reported being victims of cyberbullying and never reporting it.

Another survey conducted by NBC News that same year looked at the elderly in America. An alarming one in ten of these senior citizens had been verbally or physically abused.

School Setting Bullying

Children spend a great deal of their time at school or involved in school functions from the age of 4 or 5 to 18. During that time, they're exposed to a lot of attention from their peers, including bullying.

The U.S. Department of Education began collecting data on bullying in 2005. At that time, bullying occurred about 28% of the time. In 2014, a study showed the rate of bullying across the nation to vary from 9 percent to 98 percent! That same study reported 12-18 year olds to face bullying in the traditional sense 35% of the time and up to 15% of the time for cyberbullying.

A 2010 survey revealed 64% of children facing bullying did not report it. Much of the time, students don't think there is anyone who will help them deal with the bullying. Unfortunately, some surveys back this up.

Recent studies of schools showed, in general, policies are in place and training is available for teachers and others on how to deal with bullying. In most cases, the vast majority of school employees, (93%) know their systems have policies regarding bullying, but only a little over half (54%) have been trained in those policies.

Another national survey indicated 60% of school staff know their systems have formal bullying prevention efforts ongoing. These efforts included school teams, committees, or prevention activities. But that same survey showed less than 40% of the staff were involved in these efforts.

With these low numbers, it's no wonder students feel it's no use reporting incidents of bullying.

To be fair, the fact that school staff have many demands on their time at school must be considered. It's hard to make efforts at preventing or dealing with bullying a priority, even when staff is aware of the incidents.

It has been shown that bullying in school settings can be decreased by up to 25% when programs are put into place that are directed at stopping the practice.

It's very clear these kinds of programs are absolutely necessary in schools today. The Center for Disease Control in 2015 showed survey results that indicate fifteen and a half percent of high school students are cyberbullied and over 20% are bullied at school. The rate of bullying for middle school students is even higher. That same report from CDC showed a rate of 24% for these students being cyberbullied and 45% for being bullied at school.

From 2007 to 2016, cyberbullying has nearly doubled from 18% to 34%. Almost all (90%) of teens who have been victims of cyberbullying have also experienced bullying offline.

Students who have some sort of disability are said to be bullied two to three times more often than peers who are not disabled. The National Autistic Society reported 40 percent of children with autism and 60 percent of children with Asperger's to have suffered bullying.

The National Center for Educational Statistics in 2015 reported African-American, Hispanic, and Asian students also to be targets of bullying. Almost 25%, over 17%, and 9%, respectively for these groups.

Forms of School Bullying

There are essentially four forms of bullying that occurs in schools: verbal, social, cyber, and physical. These forms of bullying are prevalent during middle school years.

Teasing and name-calling appear to be the most frequently used forms of bullying, occurring at a rate of over 44 percent.

Rumors and lies being spread at school and over social media account for another more than 36%.

Over 32% of middle school students have been kicked, shoved, pushed, or hit by peers.

Slapping or other physical violence has been reported by over 29 percent of these students.

Almost 27.5% of middle school students have been victims of threats or theft of property.

Nearly 24 percent have been subjected to sexual gestures or comments.

A 2014 study by National Institute of Child Health and Human Development reported middle school students to have been bullied in classrooms over 29% of the time. Also reported was a 29% rate of bullying in hallways and near lockers, and almost 23.5 percent in the cafeteria.

This study shows bullying occurs in those places where student congregate. But only 20-30% of those bullied say anything to teachers or adults about the bullying.

Reasons for School Bullying

A 2009 survey by the Teen Online & Wireless Safety reported the most frequently given reasons for bullying.

Showing off for friends was given 11 percent of the time.

Fourteen percent admit wanting to be mean.

Embarrassing the victim was the reason for bullying 21% of the time.

Twenty-eight percent bullied for entertainment.

Getting back at the victim was the reason 58% of the time.

Because the victim deserved it was given as the reason 58% of the time.

Other reasons were given for bullying 16% of the time.

Effects of Bullying

Bullying has negative effects on those who bully and those who are victims of bullying. The Center for Disease Control looked at both bullies and victims, finding that those who bully are at greater risk of academic problems, substance use, and future violent behavior in adolescence and adulthood.

This same 2015 study showed students who are the victims of bullying are at greater risk of poor school adjustment, difficulty sleeping, anxiety, and depression. Along with this came the finding that those who bully and are bullied are at greater risk of developing mental health problems and behavior issues that those who are only bullied or who only bully.

A 2013 study showed students who are victims of bullying suffer more physical problems such as headaches and stomach aches than their non-victim peers. Possibly this is a reaction to the fear and distress associated with school bullying.

Those victims of bullying who blame themselves for being bullied face a greater risk of more serious problems. Maladjustment overall, depression, and continuing victimization are some of those risks.

Bullying that is bias-based or race-based leads to more serious health and mental health problems.

Workplace Bullying

In spite of contentions that bullying essentially stops once a person gets out of school, the opposite may in fact occur. A recent article in Forbes reported on a study by David Maxfield, who has been reporting on corporate culture and success since 1980.

This study found an amazing 96% of those responding said they have experienced workplace bullying. Eighty-nine percent of those doing the bullying have been at it for over a year, and 54% for more than five years! Eighty percent of the bullies affect more than five people.

The forms of these bullying episodes ranged from threatening others to sabotaging their work to physical intimidation or assaults. Many other people reported witnessing these kinds of workplace bullying.

Fifty-one percent of those responding said they knew of company policies regarding bullying, but only 7% said they knew of anyone implementing those policies.

In addition to the toll in human costs, workplace bullying is an expensive problem for companies. Recent reports have suggested in an organization of 1,000 people, one bully would cost a million dollars. Because of the multiple factors involved in trying to determine the financial costs of bullying, it may be very difficult to figure. But clearly, workplace bullying is a costly problem for companies of any size. The national financial burden of this apparently pervasive issue is likely to be astronomical.

Conclusion

The growing problem of bullying, both in schools and in the workplace, make it obvious there must be some effort made to address it. Programs and policies are clearly not sufficient in themselves to handle the problem. That makes it imperative for individuals to undertake the effort to train themselves in dealing with bullies.

A martial arts program soundly operated by a well-trained sensei is a good choice. Such a program will allow individuals of all ages to learn the self-confidence and self-discipline needed to face up to bullies at school or in the workplace. Much more will be said about this type of training later in this ebook.

What Causes Bullying?

Bullying is on the rise. According to the National Crime Prevention Council, about 60% of teens in the U.S. witness an episode of bullying daily. Reports on the television or on social media all too often tell the story of a teen who faced too much bullying and killed him or herself.

And those who do choose suicide may only be a fraction of the teens and pre-teens who fall victim to bullying daily. One source reported 99% of kids never report being cyberbullied.

No one can say bullying of one sort or another isn't a national problem. There are many programs directed at stopping and preventing bullying. Becoming aware of what causes bullying is a strong first step toward putting an end to this terrible situation.

Expected and Unexpected Causes

Nearly everyone can list the most frequently cited causes of bullying. But there are some unexpected ones, as well.

Self-esteem. Most experts in the past blamed low self-esteem for bullying behavior. They said kids who don't feel good about themselves take it out on others, making them feel miserable so the bully would feel better.

But recent research doesn't support that idea. This research shows people who are aggressive often have high self-esteem, and people who have high self-esteem aren't all aggressive. But those who are narcissistic and have high self-esteem may show significant aggression.

Those with this combination often have what researchers call unstable or fragile self-esteem. Because of this, they lash out at others who may threaten this fragile self-esteem. They are trying to defend their own highly favorable view of self from those who might tear it down.

They are doing whatever has to be done to make themselves look better. The term "selfish-esteem" has been coined to describe what these people feel.

Competition or win at all costs. Our culture fosters this kind of attitude among kids both directly and indirectly. Just go to any hometown sporting event and listen to the parents seated in the stands. This holds true from the time of the youngest tee-ball games to college level games.

Witness the open cheating prevalent in the recent Presidential election season. When confronted with this kind of cheating, one political person showed no shame at all and even stated it was okay to cheat in order to win.

How many scandals have come to light in both professional and amateur sports events where those who won have been caught cheating? These examples only set the stage for our kids to learn it's okay to do whatever is necessary to come out on top.

Bullying begets bullying. Probably the most frequently considered cause of bullying is the truth that kids who have been bullied will likely bully others. The kid who bullies likely was the victim of someone older and stronger who bullied him or her. It may not have been in the past. The bully may be bullied currently in another setting and is taking it out on his or her victim now.

This is a psychological concept called displacement. When someone bigger and stronger than you (and the bigger and stronger may be in social status, not just physical) bullies you, you can't pay them back. Thus, you find someone smaller and weaker than you and take out your anger and frustration on them.

Media Influence

There are some experts who lay a great deal of the blame for the increase in bullying, extreme bullying especially, at the feet of television "reality" programs. Many of these kinds of programs have an overabundance of aggression and hostility toward others in them. A recent study at Brigham Young University found reality programs to have nearly twice the amount of aggression, on average, than nonreality programs.

Does this model aggression as an accepted way of getting what you want, even if it is at the expense of others? Many think so. Witnessing the actors, perceived as rich and beautiful, on these programs successfully "winning" by acting aggressively may influence teens and pre-teens to behave the same way.

Psychological research would back this up. Observational or vicarious learning experiments have shown again and again that children will imitate models' behavior if those models are seen as people who are rewarded for their behavior and are physically good-looking.

It should come as no surprise, then, that some teens do whatever it takes to come out on top. This behavior seems to be increasing among teen girls. They are willing to essentially destroy others socially in order to gain or maintain their social standing. Add boyfriends into the picture, and everything is magnified.

Parents and Other Relatives

In the same way teens begin imitating so-called reality stars, they can even more imitate what they grow up with. Parents should take a close look at their own behavior when thinking about why their kids may be bullies.

If teens grow up watching and hearing their parents belittle or berate someone or some group, they will likely absorb that into their own lives. To small children, parents are perfect. Whatever they say is the truth. Whoever and whatever they like is something or someone to be liked.

And the opposite is also true. Whoever and whatever parents don't like are people and things to be avoided, to make fun of, to harass.

The same holds true for close relatives to whom a child is close or who is held in high regard by the child. What is seen, is often repeated.

Society

There are many who believe our society is becoming increasingly less civil to each other. Anyone who paid attention to the recent Presidential election season could easily agree with this. And since the election, the incivility has not diminished. If anything, it has increased.

Is this a general trend in our society? That isn't for sure at the present time. A recent poll by Weber Shandwick conducted during the recession a few years ago suggested about 65% of Americans believe a lack of civility to be a major issue across the nation. They also said this seemed to be worsened by the financial difficulties at the time.

Are things any better currently? Experience would say no.

That same poll reported, "In today's America, incivility is on prominent display: in the schools, where bullying is pervasive; in the workplace, where an increasing number are more stressed out by coworkers than their jobs; on the roads, where road rage maims and kills; in politics, where strident intolerance takes the place of earnest dialogue; and on the web, where many check their inhibitions at the digital door."

This kind of incivility daily simply adds to the stress most people feel in our society. The ever-present internet increases exposure to the lack of civility. Research indicates this continuing exposure to stress increases the chances of developing severe chronic physical problems such as coronary heart disease.

Another thing this increased stress due to incivility does is make us less tolerant of the mistakes, small or otherwise, of other people. We're less likely to be kind and more likely to exhibit anger. Anger which translates into our own less-than-civil behavior. Thus, we perpetuate the lack of civility which began this cycle of stress.

Yet another negative influence society and culture have on the development of bullies is the constant coverage by the media of explicit violent videos posing as news. This, along with the glut of realistic violence in movies, is desensitizing children and adults alike to violence and the results of violence. Thus, those who might otherwise refrain from bullying due to the impact of their behavior, no longer do so because they're used to that kind of impact from movies and television.

Adults often justify their hateful messages by citing free speech rights or values of families. Every time they do so, they are reinforcing in many children and impressionable teens the idea that bullying is all right as long as it's justified. And, by extension, the justification can be any thing the bully thinks is right or good. Anyone who is outside of those beliefs, or doesn't agree with them, becomes prey for the bully.

The attitudes of adults can be a cause of bullying, too. Many times, bullying is ignored or played down by adults because they were bullied as kids and use the excuse that the experience made them tougher. Or, they may say kids today are too soft, too easily offended or hurt, need to be tougher to survive in the world. But for most, the world is very different than when they were kids. Then, the bully only ruled parts of their life when they were away from home. Now, bullies can affect the lives of children 24/7/365.

The tendency of individuals and groups today to label those who don't agree with them as "wrong" or "not good enough" also reinforces the bullying behavior of some children and teens. Ostracizing others who don't think like you do gives some the permission to treat them differently and aggressively.

Is It Biology?

Some researchers believe there is a genetic basis for at least the foundation blocks of bullying. Is this accurate? It depends on who you believe.

Some research shows even infants spend more time staring at someone who is a different race than they do staring at someone of their own race. The researchers stated this indicates infants are paying attention to differences. But does this suggest a genetic or biological basis for future bullying of those different from them? Not necessarily.

Other researchers point to what appears to be a natural tendency to group ourselves together with others who wear the same colors. But does this suggest a future tendency to bully those who wear different colors? Who knows? There are too many other variabilities. And what wasn't reported was the presence or absence of any other factors that might have influenced children's choices.

In these and other studies purporting to show a biological basis for aggression and bullying, there were too many other possible influences that could have at least confounded the results, if not accounted for them completely. So, is there a biological basis for bullying? We still don't know.

Even if there should be proved to be this kind of biological basis, teaching kids to behave other than aggressively toward others. Raised in the right environment, any of the inherited tendencies can be overcome by children who may have them. Teaching children to enjoy differences among people and to treat others with kindness and respect will negate and keep controlled the tendencies with a biological basis.

This shows how important it is for parents to get their kids in some kind of program where self-control, self-discipline, and respect for self and others is taught directly. This kind of teaching is at the heart of most martial arts training.

Physical Bullying

When most people think about bullying they bring to mind a bigger kid picking on a smaller one. Hitting, kicking, punching, slapping are the behaviors that come to mind.

This is the kind of bullying that typically begins in middle school, although it can happen at any age. Most of the time, more boys are involved in physical bullying than girls, but this may be changing. Wanting to gain control over another person is usually the reason behind this kind of bullying.

Forms of Physical Bullying

This kind of bullying can run the gamut of behaviors from pushing and shoving to intruding on a student's personal space, all the way to physical assaults that end up with the student in the hospital.

So-called minor forms of physical bullying consist of tripping other students in the hall, bumping into others on purpose, pushing someone down, shoving them into a locker, throwing spit wads or other things at others, and hair pulling.

In themselves, these more minor behaviors may seem pretty innocuous and may even be dismissed by those in authority as merely children being children. However, they tend to add up over time, especially as they continue happening day after day to the same child. The pain and insecurity these incidents give birth to makes each of these incidents stressful and injurious.

Damaging or stealing property also are forms of physical bullying. This could range from tearing up homework projects to damaging books to tearing clothes to throwing personal property into the street or out of the bus window. Anything that destroys another student's property.

A steady progression to more serious forms of physical confrontation can happen, also. Bruises are usually the mildest of these more serious attacks. But broken bones, serious cuts, and stab wounds are possible. Some victims of physical bullying end up in the hospital or the morgue.

Some examples of physical bullying include:

- Being held against their will
- Being forced into a trash can or held upside down over a toilet
- Throwing potentially dangerous items at others
- Trying to bump someone with a car or car door as they drive by
- Gang attacks with or without weapons

While boys are typically the most physically bullying, an increasing number of girls also are engaging in physical bullying. Some researchers report 7% of girls being involved in fights every year. A steady increase in the number of girls who physically bully has been reported.

These girls engage in all of the forms of physical bullying listed above.

Physical bullying is frightening not only for the person being bullied, but also for those witnessing the act. The fear that is a major product in this kind of bullying sets the stage for all involved to have lasting negative consequences.

Sometimes, physical bullying begins as taunting or name-calling and can progress to physical intimidation and then to behaviors as terrible as torture.

Reasons for Physical Bullying

Some children seem to be born to be bullies. There are some researchers who even believe some people are born with a "bullying gene". At this point, there is no solid evidence of a genetic basis for bullying.

Bullies aren't born that way. They're made. Made by many circumstances coming together and causing kids who bully to resort to those kinds of behaviors. They victimize others to try to deal with some underlying problem in their own lives.

Some of the possible reasons for physical bullying include:

Poor examples or neglect from parents. Many case studies of physical bullying show the children who bully have been neglects by their parents. This holds true of cases from many parts of the world. Other cases show these children had parents who settled differences by violent means, or engaged in violence toward others simply for the enjoyment.

Many bullies have been bullied. More often than not, bullies who engage in physical bullying have suffered from the same attacks they commit. With the examples of aggression from parents, these children also begin thinking violence is the norm.

Schools lack supervision. Even in the best school systems, there frequently aren't enough staff available to provide sufficient supervision of students. In very large systems, this is especially true. This allows students who want to bully sufficient time and opportunity to do so.

Influence of the media. While blaming the media for everything is rampant, in this case, it appears to be warranted. There are many programs that glorify violence. These programs show those who try to be kind to others to be weak.

Peer pressure. In bullying, if your friends are engaged in the behavior, you're given open invitations to join in.

Results of Physical Bullying

The physical bruises and hurts that result from this kind of bullying certainly last, but the emotional toll lasts longer. Even if the physical bullying doesn't leave bruises, it still is very serious. This kind of bullying essentially tells the victim he or she is unliked, out of control of that which is around him or her, that he or she is surrounded by hostility, that there is nowhere safe, and that he or she is just a thing to be used for the bully's enjoyment. Actions speak loudly. And these actions are a way of delivering painful social messages. Thus, physical bullying has a strong emotional component, as well.

Signs of Physical Bullying

It's important for parents to know what to look for that can indicate their children being physically bullied. This form of bullying can end badly for the victims, therefore, it must be stopped quickly.

If you notice your child becoming withdrawn and sad, this could be the first indication of him or her being bullied. Children often won't want to do things by themselves they used to enjoy doing. They may resist going to school and even fake illness to stay home.

It's important for you to talk with them about these things.

Children who are being physically bullied often won't talk about it. They may fear getting in trouble. They may blame themselves for being bullied as a way to explain it. They may have been threatened with having worse pain inflicted if they say anything to anybody.

These victims of physical bullying learn to stay quiet. This leads them to have severe issues with trust for the rest of their lives.

Cyberbullying

The development of the internet, inexpensive cell phones, and social media has been a tremendous asset for the gathering of information quickly and for communicating directly with loved ones at the push of a button. But these same assets have become tremendous liabilities for many.

Almost instant communication with a multitude of people has opened the door to a modern form of bullying: Cyberbullying.

Bullying on social media sites and through emails or texts is on the increase. There are many types of cyberbullying, ranging from typical name-calling and teasing to much more complex forms that are very deceptive and manipulative. With only a little skill and practice, bullies can use programs like photoshop to integrate victims' pictures on very embarrassing images.

One of the most powerful aspects of cyberbullying is the number of people who can see or hear the efforts of bullies through this medium. The attacks on victims can be seen by literally hundreds or thousands of others over social media and text messages. This multiplies the impact of this kind of bullying.

The following gives an example of the impact of cyberbullying:

"When they put it on the Internet, it's like they took everything and multiplied it by an astronomical number.

It's one thing if it's a mean thing that somebody put in my school paper because that's contained within a small area. Only a certain number of people will see that. But when you put it on the Internet, you are opening it up to everyone in the world."

– Cyberbullied teen (Quoted from Kornblum, 7-15-2008)

Victims of cyberbullying often have a more difficult time dealing with it. Due to the greater number of others who have access to whatever the bully puts out on social media, the pain and psychological turmoil faced by the victim are greater.

Another reason for the tremendous impact of cyberbullying is the fact that it occurs twenty-four hours a day, seven days a week. If a child is being bullied physically he or she can get away from the tormentor for at least a short while. Going home gives this child a reprieve from being a victim, at least directly.

But a child being cyberbullied, there is no getting away. The bullying is there, no matter where he or she goes. Anywhere there is an electronic device that allows communication gives access to the hateful words.

The Different Faces of Cyberbullying

There are several ways bullies can use social media to attack their victims. It is important to understand the different varieties so parents, teachers, and others who may be able to help the victims can recognize the danger when it occurs. A major reason for this is the diversity of ways cyberbullying can take place.

Personal web pages. Many youth have their own web sites, blogs, or personal pages of some type. This makes it very easy for the cyberbully to post messages designed to hurt or slander the victim.

Re-posting emails or texts. Cyberbullies can easily re-post or forward emails or texts that were meant to be private. Depending on how "cyber-connected" the bully is, this can be seen by many other people. The embarrassment for the victim is great.

Chat rooms. Rather than face-to-face confrontation involving name-calling, chat rooms where possibly large numbers of peers gather can be used by the bully. Name-calling isn't the only thing that can go on in these chat rooms. Rumors of many kinds can also be started and/or spread in this way.

Threatening. Social media, chat rooms, and cell phones can be used to threaten or harass a victim.

Posting videos. With the huge number of cell phones in any environment, a bullying action that takes place face-to-face can be recorded by any number of people witnessing the event. This video can then be posted for viewing by anyone, significantly increasing the humiliation felt by the victim.

You Tube. Cyberbullies can make humiliating videos of what they intend to do to their victim or make up a terrible song with lyrics that embarrass the victim and post them quickly on You Tube. The intent with these videos is to threaten, intimidate, and humiliate the victim.

Posting pictures. Bullies can gain access to personal or even intimate pictures of their victims and then post them online using a computer or even a cell phone.

Taking pictures. Cyberbullies can use their cell phones to take pictures of their victims without the victim's knowledge. Most of these pictures are taken at times the victims seem to be doing something strange or looking weird. They can then be posted online with a humiliating message about the victim.

Taking the victim's identity. This form of cyberbullying can take several forms. One of these is to set up web pages or an account in the victim's name and then posting embarrassing or humiliating things on that page as if the victim is doing it. This could be a Facebook page in which slanderous things are posted in the name of the victim.

Assuming online names. Another way cyberbullies can take their victim's identity is to take over hashtags or instant message names and posting messages as if they came from the victim. These messages can serve to alienate the victim from friends and even relatives. Those who receive these messages have no idea they aren't really from the victim.

Starting services or newsfeeds. Yet another way a victim's identity can be compromised by cyberbullies is to use the victim's name to sign up for embarrassing services or newsfeeds or online publications. This can also cause the victim significant problems with his/her parents if the online information is something against the family's values or beliefs.

Making relationships. Cyberbullies can make relationships online by pretending to be someone else. The relationships will be made by the bully with the victim and are intended to embarrass and humiliate the victim. Sexting can become a part of this fake relationship. Once the sexts are sent, they then can be forwarded to many friends of the bully who will also spread them over and over.

How To Tell If Your Child Is Being Cyberbullied

These signs and symptoms of cyberbullying are taken from several web sites focusing on cyberbullying. Many of them are very similar to those signs and symptoms of bullying in general.

- If your child spends a lot of time on the computer, phone, or iPad, but doesn't say why or gives some excuse.
- If your child seems very upset or emotional after being on the computer, phone, or iPad.
- If your child seems very defensive when you ask about his or her use of the internet.
- If your child suddenly avoids or stays away from the internet.

How To Help Cyberbullying Victims

There are several things you can do to help your child who is being cyberbullied or if you are a victim of this kind of bullying.

First, you don't have to respond to a cyberbully. In fact, responding to him or her only encourages them to continue. These bullies want to know that their attacks have been successful in getting to you. So it's best not to give even the hint of validity to whatever they post or text.

Second, you always have the choice to get out of any chat room or off IM messaging when a cyberbully starts his or her attacks. These bullies are just doing this to get some kind of reaction from you. If you're not there, they will usually back off. Certainly, this won't keep them from talking behind your back, but they likely are doing that anyway. And there isn't anything you can do to stop that.

Third, if you do get texts or emails, keep them. If you have to go to the police because of the cyberbullying, you'll have these as evidence. And if you keep on getting these communications from the bully, don't get rid of or delete them. Give them to someone, authorities or parents, to hold. Besides using them if needed, you don't need to keep reading whatever the bully sends. All that does is keep making you upset.

Fourth, talk to an adult you trust. If the cyberbullying involves school, or something that happens at school, the school staff needs to know.

Fifth, parents, it's important for you to keep your response appropriate. If you forbid your child from using the internet, a phone, or other device because of cyberbullying, you're actually punishing the child twice. Be sure you place the blame for cyberbullying on the bully, not on your child or on the phone or computer.

Sixth, help your child know that most people will know whatever the cyberbully posts for what it is. Help them to know most people will look at the bully in a much worse light than they would the victim. Also help them understand the audience for these kinds of messages is very limited. There is very little chance for hundreds or thousands of people will ever see the bully's message.

Other Ways of Fighting Cyberbullying

There are other things that can be done in stopping this destructive form of bullying. Victims, families, and concerned others can use some of these approaches to bring an end to cyberbullying.

Any time a cyberbully posts something humiliating, embarrassing, or destructive, a general response can be posted. It could say something about hoping everyone who reads whatever was posted will know it was posted to bully the victim. And something about people who know this is bullying and know who the bully is saying something to him or her about how bad it is to do this.

This will help the victim understand he or she isn't alone in this situation. In addition, it will turn the tables on the bully and bring his or her actions to light.

It's possible to post responses to cyberbullying messages that can shame the bully into stopping. Talking about how people who bully must be living a difficult life by spreading lies about others. Be sure not to do the same thing the bully is doing, but stay truthful.

Flooding a chat room or other venue where damaging messages are being posted with positive messages about the victim from friends and others. Don't say anything negative about the bully, just positives about the victim.

If you see someone posting really damaging things about others on social media, say something about it. Even if you don't know the victim, stand up for him or her. It may be that just seeing someone else out there is on their side is all the victim needs to stand up for him or herself.

Conclusion

Cyberbullying is possibly the newest form of bullying. It is the most damaging due to its presence every hour of every day of every week. The anonymity of the internet adds to its damaging power. One of the best ways a victim can be helped is to get him or her into a program that will increase his or her self-confidence and self-esteem. Martial arts training will fill this need.

Sexual Bullying

While it may seem a little arbitrary to divide bullying into various "kinds," there are differences that may be important to understand if you are faced with a sullying situation. Sexual bullying is a type that appears to be prevalent among tweens and teens. Reasons for this are varied, but one possibility is the amount of attention being focused on sexuality in our culture.

Stories and news articles abound regarding "alternative lifestyles" and comments both pro and con about them. A lot of attention has been focused on males and females and their roles in society. Movies and videos are filled with explicit sexuality and sexual situations.

All of this and more contributes to an atmosphere where sex, sexuality, and references to sex are rampant. It should be no surprise to anyone that bullying would take on a sexual nature.

What Constitutes Sexual Bullying?

This is the form of bullying in which a person or a group of people focus on someone else and use sexual words, comments, and actions to attack them. This kind of bullying can quickly become homophobic in nature when the bully begins attacking the victim who appears to behave in ways contrary to his or her biological identity.

Adolescents and pre-adolescents who are just beginning to become fully aware of their sexual identity can be both giver and receiver of this kind of bullying. Uncertainty and exploration regarding sexual issues are common in this age group and can lead to some behaviors that are seen to be different that "what they should be."

Confusion over what is appropriate and not appropriate sexually may be seen also. Wonder about whether everyone feels the same way is common among kids in this age group. Widely variable sexual development can be observed in any middle school or junior high school gathering across the country.

Sexual bullying is often an invisible attack. There are no outward signs of this kind of bullying, unless the action has reached the level of physical confrontation. But the pain and damage can be lasting.

What Do Sexual Bullies Do?

The kinds of actions sexual bullies engage in are designed to humiliate and embarrass the victim. Following are some examples of sexual bullying taken from various web sites dedicated to stopping this kind of bullying.

- Using sexual jokes, comments, or gestures toward someone else
- Referring to the sexual preferences or acts of the victim
- Name-calling in sexually explicit and derogatory terms

- Becoming physical in a sexual manner by touching, pinching, or grabbing
- Brushing up against someone in a deliberately sexual way
- Posting rumors, gossip, pictures, or comments of a sexual nature online
- Sexting or manipulating the victim to engage in sexting
- Sending on to others sexually explicit tests or pictures
- Using blogs, bathroom walls, or other places to write sexual comments about victims
- Using the victim's identity online to post sexual comments

Reasons for Sexual Bullying

There are a lot of reasons why sexual bullying happens. Some of the more frequently seen reasons include wanting to gain in status in school, need for attention, and acting out against the bully's own feelings of uncertainty or inadequacy. Following are some other reasons for this kind of bullying.

A feeling of power. Like with other forms of bullying, those who engage in sexual bullying often feel powerless and inadequate. Picking on someone lower in status than themselves in a way that is guaranteed to get attention is the bully's way of gaining power. He or she can't think of any other way to get this power except to make someone else appear less than the bully. Sometimes, the feeling of powerlessness by the bully comes from his or her own bullying from another person.

To gain or re-gain control. This is control over the bully's own life. He or she may have been, or may be, in a situation where they don't have control in their life. Thus, picking someone lower in status and bullying them is a way to get control in some part of the bully's life.

To look more mature sexually. Adolescents are very concerned about their perceived sexual maturity among their peers. At times, they will go along with groups or individuals with whom they want to be identified and do things to build themselves up in the eyes of these groups. Boys seem to be more likely to engage in this kind of bullying behavior toward girls in order to be seen as more sexually mature. Girls may bully other girls as a way to decrease the victim's social status.

To get attention. For adolescents, the universe revolves around them. The more attention they can get, the better. And what better way to get attention than to tell a sexually juicy story or spread a rumor about someone else? Doing this at least gives the impression the bully knows something about the victim no one else knows.

To gain security. At times, bullies who are uncertain about their own developing sexuality and feel insecure for any number of reasons will attack someone else before they get attacked themselves. So, this kind of bullying becomes a cover-up for the bully's own feelings.

Jealousy. This is typically a reason for girls bullying other girls. It's an effort to remove the competition. Making another girl look or sound like a slut or in some other way making her appear less appealing can make the bully seem more attractive, at least in her own eyes.

Modeling others' behavior. The influence of others is great in adolescents. If a kid sees someone else bullying someone sexually, he or she may feel that influence and do the same thing. These kinds of influences can come from multiple sources: other kids, relatives, parents, or television "reality" shows.

More Thoughts About Someone Who Has Been Sexually Bullied

Many of the ways already discussed will be appropriate for those who have suffered from sexual bullying also. For parents, two things are very important: talk with your tweens and teens about sexuality, what to expect, and about your values as a family. Encourage them to talk with you or someone they trust if they have been sexually bullied.

Sexual bullying must be stopped quickly for the sake of the victim and the bully. For the victim, this kind of bullying can lead to long-lasting problems due to the intensely personal nature of the bullying. Coming as it does at a vulnerable time for young people, the impact and damage that can result may stay with them for life. In this way, sexual bullying is very similar to sexual abuse.

Depending on the timing and severity of the bullying, the victim may begin believing the lies and innuendoes that are spread about him or her. Also, the victim may begin blaming him or herself for the bullying. Either for allowing it to happen or for being so much like the bully says that someone would do this to him or her.

For the bully, this kind of behavior can be dangerous in another way. Research shows that kids who bully sexually can progress from this to sexual harassment as they grow older. This appears to be especially true of those who engage in homophobic teasing and innuendo. These behaviors seem to be predictors of future sexual harassment behavior.

Conclusion

Sexual bullying occurs at a time in the child's life when he or she is particularly vulnerable to it. This kind of bullying is damaging because of this and because the damage is emotional and not physical. Children who are the victims of this bullying suffer low self-esteem and self-confidence because they become the target of an attack on a very sensitive part of themselves.

Building self-confidence and self-esteem is a way of countering this type of bullying. Enrolling in martial arts training is an excellent way of building confidence and instilling esteem in a young person.

Effects of Bullying

There is no doubt being bullied leads to significant long-term negative effects in the person suffering the bullying. What isn't often discussed are the long-term negative effects of bullying on the one doing the bullying and on bystanders. We'll take a look at each of these three groups.

Effects on Those Being Bullied

Even though these effects have been touched on in other chapters, it's important for you to know them, so we'll discuss them here.

The negative effects of bullying on the victims are both physical and emotional. The physical effects may be something as small as bruises that come from being tripped or pushed. These go away relatively quickly. Unfortunately, there are times the physical bullying goes beyond behaviors that leave bruises. Some bullies resort to hitting and punching or even causing victims to break bones. Of course, the ultimate physical result from bullying is death. Suicides from being bullied are happening all too frequently.

The emotional effects on many victims may be even more severe. Victims of bullying are at greater risk for developing depression, anxiety, and post-traumatic stress disorder. Along with these issues, victims also develop low self-esteem and low self-confidence. When you are subjected to what seems like constant denigration and demeaning, it's not unusual to begin believing what others are saying about you.

One study investigated adults who had been bullied in childhood. The researchers found 43% of these adults said they had very low, low, or below average self-esteem. In that same study, among those who were not bullied, only 6% reported low or below average self-esteem and none among those not bullied reported very low self-esteem. This seems to provide very clear evidence of the effects of bullying on self-esteem that lasts into adulthood.

The depression that comes to victims of bullying seems to be sort of learned helplessness. They begin to feel there is nothing they can do to change things and they're doomed to go through life feeling miserable. Research suggests children who are bullied are as many as 5 times more likely to be depressed than their peers.

A feeling of sadness seems to be pervasive in children who are bullied. A study at the University of Washington School of Medicine revealed as many as 80% of bullied children feel this sadness more days than not.

There is little doubt that the effects of bullying are severely toxic psychologically. This is probably the most serious form of stress and leads to a significant feeling of being out of control. That this happens in the time of life when children are least able to handle it cognitively and rationally increases the negative effects dramatically.

At times, the victims of bullying have to find a way to relieve the inner turmoil brought on by being bullied.

They then resort to self-harm in the form of cutting or burning to get temporary relief.

A 2010 study reported in the Archives of General Psychiatry showed children bulled at age 8 to be more likely to develop psychological problems as adolescents and young adults. A 2009 study reported in the American Journal of Public Health suggested fifth graders who were bullied because of skin color to be much more likely to develop psychological disorders than their classmates.

If children have a genetic predisposition to an emotional or psychological disorder, being bullied may provide the stress needed to "turn on" those genes that cause the disorders. A British study of twelve-year-olds showed their risk of developing psychotic symptoms was more than double if they were bullied between the ages of eight and ten. If the bullying was severe and frequent, the risk tripled.

Effects on Bystanders

This group is possibly the least considered when it comes to the effects of bullying. After all, they only stand by and watch what's going on. How could they be affected by the bullying of others? The negative effects on bystanders multiplies the harm caused by bullying due to its influence on a much larger audience.

It turns out those who are exposed to others being bullied also experience some significant emotions. There is emotional pain felt by those who try to figure out what they can do to stop their friends from being bullied.

Vicarious Harm

A significant amount of research has been carried out on vicarious learning. This is the learning that takes place in others when they witness someone doing something. It is the type of encounter bystanders go through.

They may be harmed vicariously as they witness victims being bullied. The experience may be a trigger for bystanders' own insecurities. Thus, the bullying of others taps into their own sensitivities and bring significant damage.

Bullying can bring shame and insecurity to a large number of kids. No matter that those kids aren't the ones being targeted by the bully, in any group there are likely some kids who feel hurt because the taunting by the bully strikes a nerve in them because of some experience they've had or a trait they possess.

Guilt and Shame

A lot of the time, bystanders who have strong feelings of empathy will feel terrible for not standing up for the victim of bullying. There are several reasons why bystanders don't stand up for victims. One of those is fear of being singled out and possibly bullied also. Another reason is the desire to keep a relationship with the bully. And yet another is not having the social backing to make a difference.

Regardless of the reason for not intervening, bystanders who simply stand by often feel guilty for not doing something.

That this is a significant problem was pointed out by research conducted in 2002. Researchers said around 75% of the children and adolescents they surveyed reported feeling ashamed, bad, or uncomfortable watching someone get bullied. These feelings were worsened when those in authority did nothing about the bullying. When those the children relied on for security and safety did nothing, the feelings were intensified.

Fear and Anxiety

Research into trauma and its effects shows very clearly that those who witness traumatic events are just as psychologically damaged as those who are the victims of the events. This witnessing leads to anxiety, fear, and lack of security.

Similar research has shown children who witness siblings or parents being abused suffer from stress and are damaged just as much as the children who are abused. Living in a state of constant worry, fear, insecurity, conflict, and aggression leads to very significant stress.

This is the same kind of thing those who witness bullying go through. Having to stay in an environment where conflict and aggression are constant and the threat of bullying is very real has a sometimes devastating effect on all children, even if they're not being victimized.

Pressure to Participate

Bystanders to bullying may feel very significant pressure to engage in the bullying, also. Some of this pressure will be due to their desire to "fit in" with the crowd. Some may come from a usually-suppressed desire to hurt someone, too. This latter desire may not be directed at the victim of bullying, but the victim serves as a substitute for someone else.

If the bystander gives in to this pressure, later on he or she will likely feel considerable disgust directed toward self.

Effects on the Bullies

Negative effects of bullying on the bullies themselves don't typically show up until later in adulthood. During the time bullies are targeting and actively bullying others, the self-reinforcing nature of bullying keeps negative effects at bay.

However, later, the negative effects show up. One of these negative effects is getting psychologically "stuck" at adolescence. The teen years are the times when a young person is becoming his or her own person and learning how to relate appropriately to others. The bully may never progress past the need to gain power and prestige over others through bullying.

Quite a large number of possible negative effects felt by the bully may show up in later life. Among these are:

- An inability to function appropriately in social settings compared to peers.
- They may become antisocial adults.
- Decreased academic success.
- An increased risk of using drugs and alcohol.
- Violence as adults is more likely.
- This violence as adults includes domestic and child abuse.
- Their children are more at risk of becoming bullies.
- Increased risk of committing crimes and serving jail time.

In addition to the above negative effects, those who bully as children or teens are more likely to develop guilt later. This is true if the bullies engaged in the behavior for reasons other than personality disorders at an early age.

Countering the Negative Effects

Even though being bullied, witnessing bullying, or being the bully all have negative effects sooner or later, one way to counter those effects is to get the people involved in a program that helps develop self-esteem and self-control.

One of the best ways of developing these qualities is through martial arts training. Whether the child wants to progress through the different levels of martial arts or not, he or she can learn valuable personal skills that will serve him or her the rest of their lives.

Enrolling in a program run by a qualified professional will help children learn self-control, self-discipline, and self-esteem. Research and experience has shown these qualities to generalize outside of the martial arts program into all aspects of a child's life.

Basic Child and Family Safety

This chapter will cover a number of different ways kids and parents can stay safe in this sometimes chaotic world in which we live. The majority of the information will be directed toward safety online. What has been called the "new net generation" is more connected electronically than any generation before. This allows almost instant communication, which is a good thing because parents can keep in touch with their kids no matter where they are. Unfortunately, the internet also allows others to keep in touch with the kids as well.

There are multitudes of predators who surf the internet looking for their prey. With today's kids being so connected and continually on some kind of device, they are the prey.

Kids are much more trusting on the internet than those of us who have a bit more experience with life. Often, they don't think before posting significant personal information on web sites and social media. Therefore, it's important for everyone involved with kids to help them begin to understand the dangers lurking on the internet.

Stolen Identity

More and more is being said about identity theft and the terrible consequences of having your identity stolen. Some people have to spend years repairing credit after their identities were stolen online.

When someone steals another person's identity, he or she can then set up completely fake accounts and charge any number of items to those accounts. A person may only need to capture one of the following to establish these fake accounts:

- Social security number
- Bank account number
- Credit card information
- Personal information from driver's license

In addition if an identity thief gets your passwords, this can give them access to much of your information that you may not even realize can be available online.

What can you do? One very strong way of guarding your personal information online is to have and use strong passwords. Just like the best locks for your doors are complex and difficult to open without a key, your passwords should also be complex. Be sure to use a password that is complicated to others, but familiar and easy to remember for you.

Here are some tips to help you come up with strong passwords:

Always use more than one password. As tempting as it is to use the same seemingly strong password for all your accounts, don't do it! Even though it would require you to remember only one password, it also would be easier for someone to figure out that password and have access to all your accounts. Having more than one password, even if one of your accounts is compromised, the rest will be secure.

Get random, but familiar. Make your password look like a series of random numbers and characters to anyone who might see it. But also make it something that is familiar to you. For example, Myah38, may seem random to others, but mean "make yourself at home" with any numbers or characters that are meaningful to you.

Longer is better. Many, if not most, web sites where you might have an account require a password to be several letters, numbers, and characters long. Long passwords are much harder to figure out.

Make your password SUPR. (Taken from An Interactive Guide to Staying Safe on the Internet) Making your password SUPR is a way of making sure you have the best password you possibly can.

- *Strong.* Is your password strong with multiple letters, numbers, and characters?
- *Unique.* Is your password similar to your other passwords?
- *Practical.* Can you remember your password without writing it?
- *Recent.* Has your password been changed recently?

Some other steps you can take to protect yourself from identity theft and if you're a victim of identity theft:

Set up a fraud alert with any credit cards you have. This will allow the company to alert you if someone tries to use your card number. The alert typically lasts for three months. This will help if someone has used your card number already, and you want to stop the further use of the number.

Make an identity theft report. This will let your credit card companies and others know your identity has been stolen and that purchases made on the card are fraudulent. This report can stop companies from trying to collect the debt from you. It will also protect your credit score by taking false accounts off. And it will allow examination of your report to discover more about the thief.

Phishing Scams

This is the practice of using emails and harmless seeming web sites to gain access to your personal information and then using it to cause harm. You may receive emails saying that you have a refund coming to you and all you have to do is verify your information. You may not remember buying something that could lead to a refund, but everybody is interested in getting money back. And what could it hurt just to verify something? It could hurt everything! You could lose more than you can imagine.

Another scam has to do with a message saying you've won something. All you have to do is call or visit a web site and enter certain information to claim what you've won. And usually the prize is something that would be worth getting. If it were legitimate.

These phishing emails typically ask for personal information that will endanger your identity. Things like social security numbers, account numbers, birth dates, or credit card numbers. They also often have very tight deadlines by which you're told to respond. The emails may have documents attached that look very authentic. These may appear to be from banks or some other organization.

The emails aren't usually personal, so they don't have any specific information about you. If you aren't sure about the authenticity of any documents with them, call the bank or organization listed and confirm.

Another way to protect yourself from phishing scams is never to complete any forms they may send. Only give any information over secure web sites.

Never follow the links that may be embedded in these emails. This is a way for the scammer to capture your information.

Always review your credit card and bank statements as soon as you get them. Follow up on anything that looks different or isn't correct.

Scammers who use phishing emails can also fake web sites and make them look legitimate.

General Safety for the Internet

Be assured there really is no privacy on the internet. You must be careful what you post there. Anything you post will be there indefinitely and can be traced back to you.

Remember and write down everyone with whom you interact on the net. People there are often not who they say they are.

Be sure not to follow links or open emails that you aren't absolutely sure of. Don't open any files that may have been downloaded to your computer if you think they're strange, or if you're just not sure.

Be careful what you post on social media.

Parents, when do you start becoming aware of what your kids are doing on social media? As soon as they can reach the keyboard. Talk with them; tell them what can be out there on the internet. Use conversation that's geared to their understanding level. Tell them about your family values. Also inform them about what to do if they come upon a bad site.

It would be good for you to get involved on social media, also. You can ask your kids to help you set up your social media and get started.

Conclusions

There are many things you can do to protect yourself and your kids from those on the internet who would take advantage of them and do harm to them. Communication with your kids is probably the most important of the things you can do. Another is to help your kids develop the characteristics needed to resist some of these temptations. One excellent way to develop what your kids need is to enroll them in martial arts training. This will help them learn self-control, self-esteem and self-discipline. These qualities will enable them to stand up to those who would harm them over the net.

Preventive Programs to Stop Bullying

Over the recent years, there have been many programs from many groups designed to prevent bullying. Stopping bullying as it happens is good, but isn't going to make a significant difference overall. There must be a concerted effort to prevent bullying from happening in the first place.

To change a behavior that is sometimes self-reinforcing, such as bullying, would take a tremendous effort. The bully will have to want to change, something that will prove difficult with someone who has already engaged in the behavior. There would have to be some reward to substitute for the reward he or she gets from bullying. And this reward would have to be something more powerful than the reward from bullying.

If the bully decided to change for whatever reason, he or she would first have to unlearn bullying behavior, then learn more socially acceptable behavior. The process would take at least twice as long.

But if prevention is the intent, and if it is effective, this then will keep the potential bully from ever feeling the reward of bullying. Thus, he or she will only have to learn socially acceptable behavior. The process won't be as long as that described above.

The programs now being used have a number of things in common. Many of them follow the same general pattern as that taken from *www.stopbullying.gov* as listed below.

Assessment. In order to know just what a program is to target and how large an undertaking it is to be, an assessment has to be done. Surveys, interviews, and observation are some ways this kind of assessment can happen.

The importance of an assessment also has to do with finding out just how large a problem bullying is in the area. Most kids who are bullied don't tell staff or adults in the school setting about the bullying. An anonymous assessment is a way to get a more accurate estimate of the numbers of victims.

Knowing the numbers of victims and kinds of bullying taking place will help a school or organization know better the kind of prevention program to put into place. This kind of assessment should be used at various times during implementation of the program. The information gathered during these assessments will help staff and parents know how effective the program is being. It also will help them make adjustments as needed.

Get Parents and Students Involved. No one group of school staff can do everything needed to establish a preventive program to address bullying. School administrators have a great role to play in this kind of program, but it takes more.

Involving parents and students leads to students being able to focus more on learning because they're not constantly alert for bullies. They feel safer. When students feel better and learn more, parents worry less. Teachers are able to teach and do not have to monitor the behavior of the students as much. Administrators carry less of a burden of having to deal with bullies. Students will feel empowered to take a hand in what goes on in their schools.

Parents will be better able to recognize when their kids are being bullied and will be more likely to take action. Students will be encouraged to take leadership roles in these programs, leading many to seek leadership positions in other programs, as well.

Parents and school administrators can establish lines of communication that will enable more involvement in other areas of the school, as well. This communication will help both parents and school administrators stay informed regarding issues that may arise at school or at home. This allows both parties to intervene quickly if issues do arise.

Set Rules and Policies. Rules and policies set the tone for guidelines of behavior expectations and establish responses on the part of administration. These should be as comprehensive as possible in order to assure everyone knows the expectations and consequences for behavior.

Establishing a mission statement for the school sets the school's vision. Stated in various ways, this mission statement will generally outline the principles and guidelines for the school and students.

A code of conduct can help students be fully aware of the positive aspects of behaviors expected by the school. It applies to all students and teachers. It establishes standards of behavior. It outlines the positive behaviors expected of students.

A student bill of rights tells students what they can expect in the school setting. Something short and memorable is best. Letting students know they can expect a safe place to learn, can expect to be respected, and can get the help they need from caring adults.

Ensure the environment is safe and supportive. Make sure all students are welcome and included in the school. Set up a reward system for students who treat others with respect and thoughtfulness.

Monitor those places and students that have proven to be troublesome in the past. There are places of possible bullying where adults are absent for one reason or another. These are prime places for some kind of active monitoring.

All staff in the school should be actively engaged in watching for any kind of bullying behavior. Everyone in the school has contacts with students every day. Sometimes those who seem to be least in the hierarchy of education relate best with the students. Having everyone following the same guidelines with students will set the atmosphere for the school.

Education of both students and parents. Education is the school's main purpose. There is no other topic that carries any more importance than helping everyone concerned know about bullying and its consequences. The old adage, "Knowledge is power" certainly applies toward bullying. Knowing what it is, what to watch for, the consequences of the behavior, and the type of people who typically engage in the behavior will go far toward preventing it.

Education includes the positive behaviors that will aide in helping students not become victims of bullying. Behaviors such as building self-esteem, self-confidence, and self-discipline. One of the best programs in which to help your child learn these qualities is a martial arts program. A good sensei can help your child develop characteristics that will enable him or her to withstand bullies or the temptation to bully.

Self-Esteem, Self-Confidence and Bullying

One of the best ways to combat bullying is helping your kids build good, solid self-esteem. With strong self-esteem, your kids will be able to deal with bullies and will be more confident. They will learn their own strengths and how to either live with or improve their weaker qualities. And in the process, they'll learn to feel good about themselves.

In one way, this will insulate them from bullies. For the most part, bullies choose victims who are less confident and have lower self-esteem. Some bullies are very adept at picking out others who have these characteristics.

Once your kids develop strong self-esteem, most bullies will leave them alone. With good self-esteem, your kids will walk taller, hold themselves with more confidence, keep their heads up, and project an image that tells bullies they won't give in to their taunts.

Of course, there will still be some bullies who will target your kids with good self-esteem. Having the quality of strong self-esteem will help your kids withstand the taunts and other things bullies might throw their way. If your kids can ignore the bullies and not react to them, the bullies may very well leave them alone after one or two tries.

Building self-esteem and confidence will bring benefits in other ways, too. Kids with high self-esteem are at less risk of getting involved in drugs and alcohol. They will be less likely to get into relationships that end in abuse.

Following are some ways to build self-esteem and self-confidence in your kids.

Take Time For Your Kids

Spending time with your kids shows them you think they're important. Kids of all ages crave attention from parents. Giving them that time and attention will build a strong relationship with them that they can then rely on when they need strength and security. It also serves to build their self-esteem. Having this kind of foundation will encourage your kids to come to you whenever they face any of the multitude of challenges in life.

While you're spending time with your kids, give them unconditional love. Don't be afraid to hug them, kiss them, tell them you love them. They need to know you're proud of them. This doesn't mean to give them false encouragement, but do give them genuine praise for whatever they do well and work hard doing.

At the same time, let them know they don't have to be perfect. And you don't expect it. Let them also know you appreciate the effort they put forth at their various projects.

Acknowledge their good choices. And don't overdo any criticism of the bad choices they're bound to make.

Give them praise for more than just their performance in sports or academics. Praise them for doing things for others, for showing courage, taking responsibility, and for taking the lead in things.

Let Them Fail

It's important that your kids learn how to handle failure and disappointment. Letting them fail while you're in their lives to give them support and a shoulder to cry on will help them learn to deal with the feeling.

This will allow them to look at their experiences, both good and not so good, and to learn from them. Helping your kids know they can't be good at everything, but that they can deal with nearly anything will build resiliency in them.

Some parents hover over their kids and try to protect them from anything bad that might happen to them. This doesn't help them. In fact, it probably causes more harm than good. They need to know how to take reasonable risks and handle the setbacks that may come from them.

Give Them Chores and Jobs

Your kids will learn responsibility and feel the satisfaction of a well-done job when you give them chores from an early age. This lets them do something for the good of the family, also.

You're helping them develop a sense of competency which will grow their self-esteem.

Start with small chores around the house. Show them how you want the chores done, then get out of their way and let them do the work. As they get good at the small chores, give them larger and more difficult ones. As they complete the chores, praise them for the work they do and the quality of their work.

Letting them do the work themselves will let them know you believe in them. As they continue facing and handling hard chores and jobs, they begin believing in themselves, also.

Teach Them To Be Assertive

Being assertive is not the same as being aggressive. It means to stand up for themselves and realize they and their beliefs are important, too. Being aggressive means trying to force others to see and do things your way. Assertive kids have respect for the opinions of others and feel comfortable with people who see things differently.

Assertive kids will be able to say, "No!", and mean it. It's healthy to be able to do this. Your kids should know when they feel uncomfortable with something others want them to do or say, even if that person is an adult. Not doing or saying those things and being respectful when doing so is healthy.

Being assertive will also enable your kids to set good boundaries for their own and others' behavior. You should communicate your family values to them and explain why you feel the way you do about them. Helping your kids learn how to live those values is an important part of your job as parents. Live them yourself. Guard your language and behavior. Be a good example for your kids.

Help Them Learn To Insulate Themselves

No matter what your kids do, or what good things you teach them about dealing with bullies, they're going to be faced with someone calling them names at some time. You can help them learn to insulate themselves from the words others use.

This is especially important for those kids who may have some characteristic bothers them or they don't like about themselves. This is their tender spot.

Help them become less sensitive about this tender spot by talking with them about it. If there is something that can be done about whatever their tender spot may be, do it for them or encourage them to do it for themselves. While it may not be possible to rid them of the tender spot, maybe it can be made less noticeable in some way.

If there isn't anything that can be done to the tender spot, help them find examples of others who have had the same or similar things about themselves and have overcome them. It may be possible to compensate for the tender spot in some way.

It's important to help your kids learn more positive self-talk about whatever that tender spot is. Accepting it and focusing instead on some more positive characteristic can also help.

Whether or not your kids have a tender spot, it's important for them to develop the kind of insulation being discussed. Everyone will face criticism and even scorn at some time. Being able to face it and not be devastated by it will be of immense value to them throughout life.

Another Way To Build Self-Esteem

Self-esteem comes from feeling competent to deal with things that come your way. One really good way to develop this and to help your kids develop it is to get them involved in martial arts training.

Working at his or her own pace in a structured, safe environment with people who care about their success is a wonderful way to develop self-esteem. This comes as your kid learns he or she can do what is asked of them and progress in their ability to learn and apply the techniques being taught.

Getting positive feedback from others who are not family will also improve self-esteem and build self-confidence. Being immersed in a group where all are taught the same thing and all are expected to be respectful of each other will also build self-esteem.

Conclusion

Helping your kids develop self-esteem and self-confidence will not only help them deal with bullies they may encounter, but will also help them face every challenge in life with a more positive attitude.

You can help them avoid the many negative effects of being bullied by giving them the opportunity to build the qualities that will insulate them. You're not protecting them by keeping them from those challenges everyone faces. You're giving them the tools they need to be successful in facing them and handling them adequately.

Self-Discipline and Bullying

Self-discipline fosters confidence, and confidence is necessary to resist being bullied. Learning to be self-disciplined will give your kids a strong tool they can use to deal with the challenges they face in life, whether those challenges are bullies or something they really want to do right now when there is something important they must do.

Most kids are naturally impulsive. They want to do what they want at the time they want. And parents spend a lot of time and energy teaching them that isn't always possible. Some of that time and energy is also spent teaching kids to control what they say and do. That is one of the primary jobs parents have.

A lot of relationship problems can be avoided by developing self-discipline and using it.

What Is Self-Discipline?

Basically, self-discipline is learning to control yourself. Learning to control your impulses, wishes, desires, and what you do. In short, learning to control your "want to's". All of us have those things we "want to" do or say. Sometimes, it's more important not to do what we "want to."

Nothing that is good, no success, no high achievement, is attained without self-discipline. Learning to postpose immediate pleasure for the sake of a better long-term goal requires self-discipline.

In reaching any goal that is worth reaching, decisions must be made and actions taken to reach the steps that add up to that final goal. All of that requires self-discipline. There will hurdles to jump, obstacles to overcome, and people who tempt you in various ways to get sidetracked from reaching that goal.

You must learn to focus your thinking and your actions toward reaching the goal you have before you. Setting your energies and staying with the work to be done in order to achieve what you want require self-discipline. Often, you will have to set aside the opinions and actions of others in order to continue on your path to success.

And it is in dealing with the opinions and actions of others that self-discipline will help you and/or your kids deal with those who would deter you and them through the act of bullying. Your child's goal in school is to learn what is needed in order to succeed. He or she can't do that if they're subjected to bullying. With self-discipline, your child can better resist the actions and words of bullies and continue on with their learning. At work, your goal is to be the best worker at whatever you do. You can't do this if you're faced with bullying. Good self-discipline will help you deal with the bullies and continue on toward your goal of being your best.

There are several things you can do to help your child learn self-discipline. Following are a few of the activities that will help you.

Help Them Learn to Receive Correction

No one likes to be corrected. It means they've done something that didn't meet up with expectations. Kids often respond to correction either with a bad attitude or anger. Neither of these is an appropriate response that will enable them to learn from correction. It's sometimes hard for this lesson to be learned, but it will provide them a skill which will serve them well throughout their lives.

Get Them Started On Tasks That Build Self-Discipline

These tasks should begin early in your child's life. They could include taking care of a pet, running a paper route, mowing the neighbor's grass, or volunteering at a community organization. Anything that requires them to do things every time and on time would be good.

Whether or not your child earns anything from these tasks isn't the most important point. Rather, it is making sure you recognize and praise them for the self-discipline required to do the task well. Be sure to say something to your child for this. Hearing this praise from you adds to his or her feeling of competence and builds the self-discipline even more.

These tasks will also foster the quality of responsibility in your child. He or she will learn to do the right thing even if no one is watching.

Your child is building his or her character through these tasks.

Parent Cautions

Parents, remember to be patient with your children as they work to develop self-discipline. This is a procedure that takes time. Just like building their bodies to be strong takes time, so does teaching them to be self-disciplined.

If you put too much on your kids at one time, you'll likely turn them off to the idea of doing the kinds of things they must do in order to learn self-discipline. You'll also probably get a lot of resistance from your kids.

Help your kids learn what the things are that most of the time will pop up to interfere with their learning. Knowing what these are will allow your kids to avoid them or figure out ways to deal with them. Both approaches are good ways of increasing self-discipline.

Also help them learn what motivates them. Provide as many of these motivators as possible for your kids.

Enable your kids to set up routines. These can be around bed time, times for doing homework, and times to get chores done. This serves to increase self-discipline, also.

Get your kids in touch with others who have developed the self-discipline to achieve good or even great things.

This can be through books and videos, as well as in person.

Help your kids learn to visualize reaching their goals. If they can get in mind what it will be like to finally achieve what they desire to do, it will become a strong source of attraction pulling them to their goals continually.

A Great Way To Develop Self-Discipline

Getting your kids involved in martial arts training is an excellent way to develop this characteristic that will serve them well throughout life. Learning to stay with the practice required to become good at this sport will teach them self-discipline. And this quality will help them in all areas of their life, not just martial arts.

With this training, your child will be better able to stay with other projects that he or she has to complete. It will also give them the confidence they need to try new things and do their best working at them.

This will help them learn self-control, giving them the ability not to act on impulse, but to think things through before acting.

Self-discipline is the foundation for developing self-confidence and self-esteem. These are two of the best qualities for your children to have to enable them to deal with bullies.

The Importance of Parenting and Communication

Parents, you have an extremely important and difficult job to do. And, unfortunately, a part of that job is helping your kids deal with bullies.

Nearly all kids who attend school will face bullying, either as a victim or a bystander. Bullying is almost reaching the point of epidemic in our school systems. There are many negative effects of bullying, either for the victim or the bystander. Whatever parents can do to help their kids handle any bullying that may come into their lives.

Here are some things you as parents can do to help your kids deal with bullying.

Help Them Learn About Bullying

This means first of all you must learn about bullying. What it looks like, where it happens, the results of being bullied. Then, you can talk with your kids about it.

Knowing what bullying is will help your kids recognize it when it happens to them or one of their friends. When they recognize bullying, they can talk about it. Talk about it with you or with a trusted adult. And that it's okay to tell adults about bullying when they see it.

Let them know, also, it's okay to help others who may be bullied. They may not intervene directly, but giving the other kid support and helping them find adults to talk to may be better.

Always Communicate

Remember, your kids operate on a different wave length than you do. You can't always tell when they're ready to talk or listen. But you should always be ready to talk and listen when they are.

Sit down one-on-one with your kids and talk. Research shows kids do depend on parents and other adults for guidance and advice on what to do in a lot of situations. They may not tell you that and may even resist talking at first. Stay with it! They will appreciate you, even if they don't show it.

Spend a definite amount of time with your kids frequently. When you're with them, pay attention to them only. Get rid of all other distractions. Keep eye contact, but not constantly.

Start your sessions with your kids slowly and with questions about neutral things, like school and favorite things they do. As your kids get more comfortable with the idea of talking about things, you can introduce other topics that may be more serious.

At some point, you'll want to bring up the topic of bullying. At the same time you're talking about the issue, encourage your kids to ask questions. Keep in mind you may not have an answer. Or there may be no right or wrong answer. That's okay. One thing you can do is share your opinion and then ask your kid for his or her opinion.

There are web sites that can give you suggested questions to encourage discussion.

Listening: The Forgotten Skill

Many parents tend to do a lot of talking and not much listening when trying to communicate with their kids. Listening is possibly the more important part of communication. Learning to listen, really listen, to your kids show them how important they are to you.

You learn more by listening than you do by talking. You'll get a better understanding of what your kids are going through, which will give you more information to base your opinion and advice on. You also get a good idea about what your kids think about situations.

Listening also helps you avoid confusion and misunderstandings. This will keep you from getting into conflict with your kids at a time when you're working to form stronger relationships with them.

Body Language

The best communicators know how important body language can be when you're trying to talk with your kids. Body language can actually communicate deeper feelings than any words can. And often others will respond to body language in place of what you say.

Body language includes facial expression, body position, gestures, eye contact, and tone of voice. All of these are especially important to keep in mind when you're talking about topics that are difficult or have a lot of emotion with them.

Some examples of positive body language include:

- Keeping your body open. This means not crossing your arms or your legs. Be aware of your facial expression; be sure not to frown.
- Be sure you face whoever you're talking to. Lean a little close, sit close if your kids will tolerate it.
- Make sure you keep eye contact. Not all the time; this can be felt to be threatening to some kids. And tolerate little or no eye contact from them.
- Nod your head when others are speaking. This lets them know you're hearing them.

Don't Over-React

You're going to hear some things that you're not going to understand and not going to like. Especially when those things have to do with your child telling you about being bullied or witnessing someone else being bullied.

It's important not to over-react. You may be tempted to show your temper against what has happened. Don't give in to this.

It's just as important for you not to under-react. In other words, don't be so passive when your child finally gets up the courage to say something about bullying that he or she gets the idea you don't really care.

Keep in mind home is your child's refuge if he or she is being bullied. Knowing you care and want to help him or her makes home even more of a safe and protected place.

Some Other Parenting Helps

There are quite a few other things you can do to help your kids deal with bullying.

Teach your kid some ways to handle bullies. Never tell them to hit back or taunt back. This is completely unacceptable. Many schools have a zero tolerance policy regarding bullying. If your kid hits or bullies back, he or she will also get in trouble.

Instead, teach them to report bullying, whether they're being bullied or see someone else being bullied. Let them know it's okay to walk away from someone trying to bully them, if they can.

If your child is being bullied on the way to or from school, help him or her find a safe place along the way where they can go if they're chased by a bully. Arrange for him or her to be able to call a trusted adult if afraid the bullying is going to get physical. Encourage them to find an adult or older student to walk with.

Encourage your child to make new friends and get a fresh start that way. Help them pick out some other kids that might make friends who would be good for them. Be careful about this. Some kids don't want anyone to think their parents are picking out their friends. Make suggestions, but remember it's your kid's life, and he or she needs to make these decisions.

What About The Parents Of Bullies?

If you find out your child is a bully, there are some things you can do to help him or her make changes.

First, be aware of your own attitudes and actions. Are there some times you voice negative comments about others? Do you make jokes about people who are different from you? Even if these are done or said in jest, they set the stage for your kids to do the same thing, but more seriously.

Next, be sure to treat the situation seriously. Don't just dismiss your child's behavior as not meaning anything or as something just like you used to do. This can be a very serious event in your child's life. One that can determine a lot of his or her future.

It's also important for you to be sure you have all the facts in the situation. Listen to your child, but also talk with others about what happened. Talk with your child about reasons for his or her behavior. Don't blame or threaten.

Be sure to hold your child responsible for his or her actions. Make it clear that his or her decisions have consequences, either negative or positive. Don't take the blame for his or her behavior yourself.

Communicate to your child the rules of conduct in your family. Consequences for breaking the rules should be non-hostile and consistent. Be sure to give much praise for following the rules.

Many parents still use corporal punishment as a consequence. This likely won't work if your child is a bully. Rather, it will just reinforce his thinking that it's okay to use force on others.

Enlist the help of the school to provide negative consequences there, also. This may speed up your child's changing behavior.

Spend time with your child. Time doing things he or she enjoys. Encourage them to talk to you about things going on in their lives.

You may find out there is something serious going on in your child's life. Don't be slow to seek professional help if your child needs it. This may be a significant way to help your child make changes.

All kids can benefit from being involved in a program that fosters respect, self-discipline, and self-esteem. This kind of program can be found in martial arts training. The qualities a kid needs to succeed are taught there. Those who are bullied as well as those who bully can benefit from this kind of training under a well-qualified professional.

The Benefits of Martial Arts Training

Throughout this book the importance of developing the qualities necessary to resist bullying and to overcome the effects of bullying have been mentioned. One of the best arenas for developing these qualities is the home, of course. Parents are the very best teachers for their children.

There are programs available to help parents in teaching their kids these qualities. One of the best for developing the specific essential qualities kids need is martial arts training.

There is no better place for your child to learn how to relieve the stress he or she may experience from being bullied or witnessing bullying. No better place for your child to get into the best physical shape of his or her life and to ingrain this desire to stay in shape. No better place for him or her to learn self-confidence by learning defensive techniques to help ensure safety.

One intent of martial arts training is to condition both mind and body to function optimally. The need to stay focused and alert conditions the mind as the movement and practice condition the body.

Welfare of each student is uppermost in the minds of the instructors in martial arts training. Not only are they concerned about safety and training in the various martial arts techniques, but also in the development of the student's character.

The insistence on respect, following directions, courtesy, waiting for your turn, and dedication to practice are all designed to build character. These character traits will then generalize to other parts of your child's life. This has been shown through research to be true.

Good self-discipline and stronger self-esteem will grow as your child progresses through the program. He or she will see the difference in self, and others will comment on the changes as well. This boosts self-esteem and confidence.

"What will this do for my child's experiences with bullies?", you may ask.

It will give him or her the self-confidence to avoid bullies if at all possible. If not possible to avoid them, your child will have self-esteem strong enough to ignore the taunts bullies may hurl at them. It is even possible for your child to gain the poise needed not to project the image of someone who can be bullied.

Often, bullies have the ability to pick out those who can be bullied. The shy, timid child who looks at the floor as he walks the halls will become a target. But your child, who has learned to walk with head held high and eyes taking in everything, will be seen as someone who likely won't tolerate being bullied.

Will your child learn the skills needed to defend him or herself if needed? Yes. But more important, he or she will learn not to retaliate physically because of being self-controlled. He or she will be confident enough to talk with those adults who can do something about the bullies in his or her life.

Martial arts training will give your child the qualities needed to meet the challenges of life from now on. Whether those challenges be bullies at school, some physical challenge requiring strength and confidence, or some challenge in the workplace later in life, your child will know how to deal with them.

You want the best for your child and are willing to do whatever you can to give him or her the skills and qualities needed to succeed. Martial arts training can help you in providing these skills and qualities.

Take Action

One of the most powerful things you can do is to constantly raise the confidence levels of your child. To give him/her skills to deal with the world, as it is, not as we all wish it was. Martial Arts training can have a lasting positive impact in all areas of life. Martial Arts training is something your child can do all year round.

About Edward Carr

Edward Carr has owned Tokyo Joe's Studios of Self Defense for over 20 Years.

His Studio is Located at 1338 Hooksett Road, Hooksett, N.H 03106.

He can be reached at 1-(603)-641-3444 or at *tokyojoeshooksett@comcast.net*.

Web site is *https://tokyojoeshooksett.com*

Feel free to contact him and see how to take advantage of a free 2 weeks of training in all classes.

Biography

Edward Carr

As owner and head instructor, Ed Carr has operated Tokyo Joe's Studios since day one, working to cultivate a team of talented and professional martial artists under his banner. Ed has over 30 years of martial arts experience, holding a 5th Degree Black Belt in Kempo Karate, a Brown Belt in Brazilian Jiu-Jitsu, many years experience as a sport karate fighter, and a professional MMA fighter(4-1) as a member of the world famous MFS fight team. Some of his accomplishments include being a 3x Krane National Karate Champion, IBJJF Pan-Am Purple Belt Champion, IBJJF Boston Open Champion and being entered into the U.S.A. Martial Arts Hall of Fame for Kempo Instructor of the Year. Ed Carr has devoted his time and life to bettering the lives of his students through martial arts.

www.ingramcontent.com/pod-product-compliance
Lightning Source LLC
Chambersburg PA
CBHW020017050426
42450CB00005B/518